# SUMMARY of MINDSET

## The New Psychology of Success

### by Carol S. Dweck, Ph.D.

*A FastReads Book Summary with
Key Takeaways & Analysis*

Copyright © 2017 by FastReads. All rights reserved. This book or parts thereof may not be reproduced in any form, stored in any retrieval system, or transmitted in any form by any means—electronic, mechanical, photocopy, recording, or otherwise—without prior written permission of the publisher, except as provided by United States of America copyright law. This is an unofficial summary for educational purposes and is not intended as a substitute or replacement for *Mindset*.

# TABLE OF CONTENTS

**EXECUTIVE SUMMARY** .................................................................................... 4
**INTRODUCTION** ............................................................................................... 5
**CHAPTER 1 *THE MINDSETS*** ........................................................................ 6
   Why Do People Differ?
   What Does All This Mean for You? The Two Mindsets
   A View from the Two Mindsets
   So, What's New?
   Self-Insight: Who Has Accurate Views of Their Assets and Limitations?
   What's in Store

**CHAPTER 2 *INSIDE THE MINDSETS*** ........................................................... 8
   Is Success About Learning-Or Proving You're Smart?
   Mindsets Change the Meaning of Failure
   Mindsets Change the Meaning of Effort
   Questions and Answers

**CHAPTER 3 *THE TRUTH ABOUT ABILITY AND ACCOMPLISHMENT*** ................................................................................. 10
   Mindset and School Achievement
   Is Artistic Ability a Gift?
   The Dangers of Praise and Positive Labels
   Negative Labels and How They Work

**CHAPTER 4 *SPORTS: THE MINDSET OF A CHAMPION*** .......................... 12
   The Idea of the Natural
   "Character"
   What is Success?
   What is Failure?
   Taking Charge of Success
   What Does It Mean to Be a Star?
   Hearing the Mindsets

**CHAPTER 5 *BUSINESS: MINDSET AND LEADERSHIP*** .......................... 15
   Enron and the Talent Mindset
   Organizations that Grow
   A Study of Mindset and Management Decisions
   Leadership and the Fixed Mindset
   Fixed-Mindset Leaders in Action
   Growth-Mindset Leaders in Action

A Study of Group Processes
Groupthink Versus We Think
The Praised Generation Hits the Workforce
Are Negotiators Born or Made?
Corporate Training: Are Managers Born or Made?
Are Leaders Born or Made?

## CHAPTER 6 *RELATIONSHIPS: MINDSETS IN LOVE (OR NOT)* ...... 19

Relationships Are Different
Mindsets Falling in Love
The Partner as Enemy
Competition: Who's The Greatest?
Developing Relationships
Friendships
Shyness
Bullies and Victims: Revenge Revisited

## CHAPTER 7 *PARENTS, TEACHERS AND COACHES: WHERE DO MINDSETS COME FROM?* ........ 21

Parents (and Teachers) Messages About Success and Failure
Teachers (and Parents): What Makes a Great Teacher? (Or Parent)
Coaches: Winning Through Mindset
Our Legacy

## CHAPTER 8 *CHANGING MINDSETS* ........ 23

The Nature of Change
The Mindset Lectures
A Mindset Workshop
Brainology
More About Change
Taking the First Step
People Who Don't Want to Change
Changing Your Child's Mindset
Mindset and Willpower
Maintaining Change
The Road Ahead

# EXECUTIVE SUMMARY

It's rare that a self-help book presents a truly groundbreaking idea, but that is exactly what Carol Dweck, Ph.D. implies in *Mindset: The New Psychology of Success*. It's been working wonders for her graduate students every year, and through this book, she is bringing her research to a wider audience.

After going through decades of personal research on achievement and success, Dr. Dweck has concluded that the most important variable for achievement and success comes from the power of our mindset.

In *Mindset,* Dr. Dweck shows the reader how it's more than abilities and talents that bring success, it's how they view the world. She makes a clear distinction between fixed and growth mindsets and shows the ways that a specific mindset changes how we confront challenges, whether we are four-year-olds or graduate students. In her view, praising intelligence and ability doesn't create self-esteem or lead to accomplishment; in fact, it's one of the most damaging things a parent can do for their children's ability to succeed!

By learning to adopt the proper mindset, Dr. Dweck teaches us that we can become better parents, teachers, athletes and even CEOs. It's just as simple as controlling the potential that we have in our own minds.

# INTRODUCTION

Professor Dweck wrote this book at the request of her students. They found the material that she was teaching to be so engaging and eye opening to their own lives that they wanted her to bring it to a larger audience. With their persuasion, *Mindset* was written.

In this book, Professor Dweck outlines the ways that a simple belief about your own potential changes the ways you run your life. She argues that your mindset about your potential to grow from experiences permeates every part of your life and affects how well you are able to grow from successes and failures.

For the first time, she presents the psychological research that transformed her life and her student's life to a greater audience.

# CHAPTER 1
## *THE MINDSETS*

## Why Do People Differ?

Even kids differ in the ways that they view themselves. When given both an easy and difficult puzzle to solve, some will be content to stay with the easy one and never attempt the hard one, while others will spend hours trying to tackle the difficult one. Some kids are afraid of looking stupid so they decide not to try hard, while others do everything they can to learn how to take on harder challenges.

What causes this difference in personality? It is based on the shape of your skull? Genetics? Background? Supportive home environments? Science has been debating this idea for centuries without coming to a strong conclusion.

Today, most researchers agree that both nature and nurture affect the way we view ourselves, but the ways that our views can change over time is still debated.

## What Does All This Mean for You? The Two Mindsets

Dweck's research has shown for twenty years that 'the view you adopt of yourself profoundly affects the way you lead your life.' In short, a simple mindset about your abilities is a key indicator of how much you will manage to accomplish in life. Professor Dweck presents two main mindsets that people adopt: the fixed mindset and the growth mindset.

**Fixed Mindset:** A belief that your personal qualities are innate and set in stone- you are born with a certain level of intelligence and the rest of your life is an opportunity to prove it to others.

**Growth Mindset**: A belief that your basic qualities are cultivated through effort. You believe that your true potential is unlimited and depends on how you apply yourself in different situations, which gives you a passion for stretching yourself and sticking to it for difficult problems.

## A View from the Two Mindsets

Imagine going through a terrible day, one where you get a bad grade from a professor and then find a parking ticket on your car. How would you respond? The two mindsets cause people to respond in different ways to this situation.

In the fixed mindset, you blame yourself and sink into a minor depression. You assume your teacher is out to get you, that you're not smart enough to do well, that you're an idiot for parking illegally. The chance that you would do anything to fix the situation is minimal.

In the growth mindset, you would be justifiably upset, but starting thinking through the next steps. You would plan to study harder for the next test and possibly challenge the ticket in court. Though you'd be upset, you would find ways to move the situation forward without labeling yourself from it.

## So, What's New?

This may not seem ground breaking to you, but Dr. Dweck's research has shown that the ability to move on from personal failures comes directly from the growth mindset. You can read dozens of books by successful entrepreneurs, but without thinking about their advice through the importance of mindset you won't be able to make it applicable for your life. Understanding how mindset affects your actions will teach you the importance of controlling your mindset.

## Self-Insight: Who Has Accurate Views of Their Assets and Limitations?

Just because you have a growth mindset doesn't mean you are actually more in control of your abilities, does it? Actually, research has shown that people with a growth mindset are better able to estimate their abilities and know what they are capable of. This is because the belief that you can develop yourself implies that you have work to do, which is why growth mindset people are better able to be realistic about their weaknesses.

## What's in Store

Growth mindset people also have a knack for turning their setbacks into later success. They understand that they are works in progress, while fixed mindset people get caught in the trap of proving their own intelligence by never encountering anything that will undermine it. Later chapters will expand on this mental switch more and teach you ways that you can maximize your own mindset for growth.

## *Key Takeaways*

- The different ways that people view the world affect the ways that they chose to interact with it.

- A "fixed mindset" view of the world makes you risk averse and preoccupied with proving your abilities.

- A "growth mindset" view allows you to see challenges as steps towards progress and a way to improve yourself.

- The mindset you adopt will have huge effects on your long term success and accomplishments.

# CHAPTER 2
## INSIDE THE MINDSETS

## Is Success About Learning-Or Proving You're Smart?

Watching children wrestle with the limits of their intelligence is an interesting way to study the two mindsets in action. Fixed mindset children are more interested in proving themselves than learning, and they shy away from difficult puzzles that may cause them to fail, proving that they have flaws in their intelligence. In contrast, growth mindset children happily tackle difficult problems and get excited about the opportunities to learn. A study showed this principle when foreign college students were offered opportunities to take extra language classes to help them improve before starting class. Fixed mindset students refused the classes for fear of looking unintelligent, though they were the best way to become MORE intelligent in the future. Growth mindset students happily signed up for the classes because they understood it would help them in the future.

## Mindsets Change the Meaning of Failure

In a fixed mindset, failure becomes a huge problem. Children go to extremes to avoid it, even if it means they don't challenge themselves. Failures come to define people in the fixed mindset and they can't think of their value as separate from them. Achieving success becomes important at all costs, even if it requires cheating, assigning blame, making excuses and breaking the rules.

Growth mindset people don't exactly enjoy failure, but it makes them less miserable because they don't define so much of their worth by it. They understand that the path to success will have failures along the way and they are comfortable facing them, so long as there are opportunities to learn along the way.

## Mindsets Change the Meaning of Effort

Think of the story of the tortoise and the hare. Who do you want to be in that story? In all honesty, most of us strive to be a less stupid hare. We want to succeed quickly without plodding effort. A story like this provides the mentality that people either have the natural ability OR have to put forth lots of effort. Rarely do we hear about the talented person that still had to work incredibly hard to succeed.

As a society, we love stories of natural, effortless accomplishments. Frankly, this mindset is both unrealistic and damaging because no success is effortless and often requires a level of failure.

## Questions and Answers

Dr. Dweck clears up confusion about the mindsets by restating the importance of confidence and an ability to see failures as separate from your overall self-worth.

## *Key Takeaways*

• Failure is only bad if you let it define your worth.

• No success comes without effort, and pretending otherwise might prevent us from trying our hardest.

• Looking like a failure in the short term in order to try something that challenges you is the best way to set yourself up for success in future.

# CHAPTER 3
# *THE TRUTH ABOUT ABILITY AND ACCOMPLISHMENT*

It's easy to think of historical figures like Edison and Darwin working by themselves until they stumbled upon genius discoveries because of their natural brilliance. But in actuality, both of these men devoted years of hard effort to their work and had a supportive team behind them to help along the way. Even Mozart had to write a lot of terrible music before creating his brilliant symphonies.

## Mindset and School Achievement

School children suffer during transition times when they operate under the fixed mindset. It causes their grades to plummet when they start high school because they feel that having to work hard means they don't have natural talent. They also find it easier to blame outside circumstances (like their teachers) for their problems. In essence, the fixed mindset limits student's achievement.

Growth mindset students are more likely to apply themselves to difficult problems and put in the hard work to succeed. They don't define themselves by their natural intelligence, so they are willing to push themselves harder, which causes them to learn better study strategies that help them to keep progressing to higher levels of achievement.

## Is Artistic Ability a Gift?

The idea that artistic talent is only a natural ability is subject to critique. When people are given a few drawing classes, their abilities skyrocket and their work improves dramatically. The lesson is simple. Just because some people can do something with minimal training, this doesn't mean that others can't do it if they try hard enough to learn how. Jackson Pollock, for example, had little natural talent for art but he was so passionate that he managed to become innovative and a master.

## The Dangers of Praise and Positive Labels

It might seem obvious that artistic ability should be viewed as a gift, but this isn't always the case. Having natural talent can put such extreme expectations on children that they fear not living up to their potential. Playing the violin becomes a chore, not a passion. In fact, children can become so concerned about performing to the standard that has been set for them that they are willing to lie about test grades in order to seem more accomplished.

In contrast, when children are praised for their efforts rather than their intelligence, they are much more likely to work towards bigger challenges.

# Negative Labels and How They Work

Societal stereotypes can have a big impact on success. When girls are reminded that they "aren't as good at math as boys" their test scores plummet. The same holds true for African American students and even Asian students (but in the other direction- when they are reminded that they are Asian their test scores improve!) What causes this phenomena? The fixed mindset belief of skills. Growth mindset thinkers are less susceptible to these stereotypes because they don't see their abilities as set in stone.

The best way to help girls and minorities get more involved with science and math majors in college is to foster a growth mindset of unlimited abilities.

## *Key Takeaways*

- The way that students view their intelligence will have big impacts on their overall successes.

- Artistic ability is less dependent on natural skills, but rather is something that can be learned and improved.

- Reminding students of damaging stereotypes will cause them to prove them true through decreased performance on tests.

- People can do a lot more than meets the eye, if only they decide to apply themselves.

# CHAPTER 4
## *SPORTS: THE MINDSET OF A CHAMPION*

## The Idea of the Natural

Natural talent is so revered in sports that there is little acceptance for anything else. This might be because physical abilities are so obvious compared to mental ones- you can actually see the height and rippling muscles on a talented basketball player as opposed to the brains of a mathematician.

However, the reverence for the natural is often overstated. Muhammad Ali was anything but a boxing natural, yet he became one of the most celebrated boxers of all time. Even Michael Jordan was cut from his high school team before he took his playing seriously and spent hours practicing every day. For both these athletes, mental toughness and strength became far more important than the physical abilities they had naturally- and mental toughness can only be strengthened through the growth mindset.

These athletes would scoff at the idea that naturals don't need to work hard for success. Instead, what sets them apart is how incredibly hard they worked to get where they were.

## "Character"

Perhaps more important to these athletes than their natural abilities were their character and ability to focus on constant improvement. "Natural" athletes don't need to learn to overcome failure, so they don't learn the mental toughness for fighting it.

Character is what underdog teams have, teams that have to scratch their way up from the bottom and are grateful for every point they can get. They are scrappy and opportunists, and they take advantage of every situation that comes their way. Rather than resting on the confidence of their past successes, they operate with eyes wide open in pursuit of new opportunities to learn and grow.

Tournament winners often aren't the best athletes. They are the ones that try the hardest and are most willing to stretch themselves beyond their normal abilities.

## What is Success?

An athlete's mindset changes the ways that they define success. A growth mindset causes them to define success as doing their best and constantly learning and improving. For a fixed mindset athlete, success only comes from winning-- everything else is a failure.

## What is Failure?

Growth mindset athletes see failure as a giant wake up call. Failures are opportunities for learning from mistakes and are motivation for improving in the future. Fixed mindset athletes view failure as a personal attack on their abilities and natural talents, and they will do anything possible to shift the blame from themselves, whether through blaming the weather or the refs. If these excuses fall short, fixed mindset players often fall into depression.

## Taking Charge of Success

Athletes with a growth mindset almost inevitably take control of the process that brings them success and continuously adapt it to fit their current situation. Michael Jordan didn't decline with age because he kept finding ways to match his techniques to the realities of his body. Tiger Woods' dad did everything he could to distract his son on the course in order to develop his resolve and focus during tournaments.

Fixed mindset athletes don't take control of their abilities in the same way. They depend on their talent to coast them through and refuse to see themselves as a work in progress. If they don't win, they comfort themselves with the knowledge that there was nothing else they could do- even if this is far from the truth.

## What Does It Mean to Be a Star?

Being a star means different things for different mindsets. Fixed mindset athletes need to constantly validate their talents, which means they need to see themselves as a superstar, not just a team player.

In contrast, growth mindset players know that success comes from the efforts of the whole team, not just them. They are willing to take positions that aren't best suited for them if it benefits the rest of the team, and they find more validation in team victories than personal success.

## Hearing the Mindsets

The mindset that an athlete has is obvious from the beginning, long before they go pro. Fixed mindset athletes will be razor focused on perfection and refuse to accept anything less from themselves. They will see success as critically essentially for turning them from a "nobody" to a "somebody", because all self-worth comes from a demonstration of their inner talents.

Growth mindset players are always watching and observing and trying to learn. They want to win just as badly as fixed mindset players, but they don't fear loss in the same way, and they don't attach all their self-worth to their performance. Instead, they play the long game and find success from the knowledge that they are constantly improving.

## *Key Takeaways*

• All athletes want to win, but fixed-mindset players see it as critical for revealing their self-worth.

• The growth mindset helps star athletes become better team players.

• In the growth mindset, failure becomes an opportunity for improving, not an exposure of your natural ineptness.

# CHAPTER 5
# BUSINESS: MINDSET AND LEADERSHIP

## Enron and the Talent Mindset

When Enron went bankrupt in 2001 it shocked the corporate world. Enron had built its reputation on hiring the best talent it could find and it reveled in that talent. How was failure possible?

In fact, the "talent mindset" of Enron was the company's downfall. By recruiting fancy degrees and paying them big money to achieve, Enron put all its faith in creating a culture that worshiped talent, even at the expense of actual achievements. Looking brilliant became more important than doing brilliant things, and Enron forced its employees into a fixed mindset way of thinking that never created space for questioning the process or correcting problems along the way.

As it turns out, a company that can't self-correct won't manage to be a company for long.

## Organizations that Grow

Not all companies get caught in the fixed-mindset talent trap. In many ways, the key to long term growth-minded success for companies was found in the leadership. Self-effacing people that asked questions without fear of confronting brutal answers were able to move forward from failures by correcting along the way, which lead their company to sustained success.

In essence, successful leaders need to operate with the growth mindset.

## A Study of Mindset and Management Decisions

Studies that place company managers in specific mindsets to see how they react consistently reveal that the growth mindset is the best way for them to motivate their employees to achieve. When people are told that their management skills are based on their natural abilities, they are less likely to lead effectively or put themselves in situation where they might be wrong, which could cause them to challenge their natural talents. They will shy away from challenges, while those that were primed with a growth mindset by being told that management skills develop with practice went out and practiced.

At the end of the studies, growth mindset managers proved to be far more productive than fixed mindset ones, and their employees were happier as well!

## Leadership and the Fixed Mindset

Fixed mindset leaders tend to be obsessed with their "reputation for personal greatness" which caused them to set up their company to fail in their absence. In fact, this was often the goal, because having their company become completely dependent on their input became proof of their own personal greatness and need.

Likewise, fixed leaders don't work with teams. Instead, they have "little helpers" that help them to show off their skills. They need to be the biggest fish in the pond, and anyone that comes close to their level of talent and ability is a threat, not an ally.

The power that a fixed mindset leader has is used to as a display for others, not as a way to operate a better business.

## Fixed-Mindset Leaders in Action

Fixed mindset leaders are threatened by the talent surrounding them, not encouraged. When Iacocca, the CEO of Chrysler Motors, saw that his employees were creating innovative car designs, he refused to approve them for fear that they would get all the credit and leave him looking inferior by comparison. His fixed mindset towards progress and obsession with his own professional image caused him to drive Chrysler into the ground as foreign markets began to snatch up their market share.

CEOs can live in bubbles of their own making, surrounding themselves with people and facts that are testaments to their perceived brilliance. Because of this, deep-seated issues that can cause bankruptcy often catch them completely by surprise.

## Growth-Mindset Leaders in Action

In contrast, growth leaders put the good of their company ahead of their personal desires to achieve. Growth mindset leaders are willing to ask the hard questions, listen to the honest answers from those around them, and even fill their staff with people whom are more talented than them. It becomes less about boosting their own self-image and more about making decisions for the good of the company.

Growth mindset leaders don't see their work as an opportunity to laud honor on themselves. Rather, it is a marathon filled with careful decisions to achieve the end goals that are far in the distance. They value the passion and ability for growth in their employees more than their innate talent. And because of this mindset, they achieve fantastic results.

## A Study of Group Processes

Studies have shown that group projects with growth-minded people tend to produce more exciting, innovative solutions than fixed-minded people who are too afraid of failing to try to stretch themselves.

## Groupthink Versus We Think

Groupthink happens when people start to think alike without anyone taking a critical stance. It happens around charismatic leaders, often with devastating results. The Bay of Pigs invasion was a terrible idea, but not one member of President Kennedy's staff was willing to stand up against it, so convinced were they of their leader's luck and brilliance.

The best leaders seek out dissent and listen to it. A variety of opinions makes it easier to make the best overall decision, and they take advantage of it. Leadership isn't viewed as faultless gods, but rather as human beings with opinions just like everyone else.

## The Praised Generation Hits the Workforce

What happens to society as "participation medal" millennial adults enter the workforce? This generation has been praised since birth and is filled with over-healthy self-esteem about how talented and special they are. This is becoming a huge issue in the workforce as employees strive to pile on praise and shy away from any criticism that might damper the spirits of their young workers.

It seems that the parents of millennials have dropped the ball in developing a healthy growth mindset, so employers might need to pick up the slack and teach their workers how to handle constructive criticism.

## Are Negotiators Born or Made?

Negotiations are critical for success as a business person, but are negotiators born or developed? As it turns out, people that are told that negotiators can develop through intensive practice are more willing to take risks and work harder to become better, where people who are told that negotiation is a fixed trait aren't willing to try as hard to prove themselves.

Overall, having a growth mindset causes negotiators to do almost twice as well as those with a fixed mindset.

## Corporate Training: Are Managers Born or Made?

Millions of dollars are spent each year trying to improve the effectiveness of leaders, but does it really help? Not really; in most cases bad leaders continue to be bad, no matter what training they are exposed to. However, few of them are ever exposed to the growth mindset, and a change in mindset can make a huge difference in their overall effectiveness as leaders.

Fixed mindset managers look for existing talent and make snap decisions about their employees, quickly writing off the ones that they don't think have potential. This causes them to narrow their focus on a select few, often missing out on talent that could be developed within their staff.

Growth mindset managers think talent is a nice starting point, but that it means nothing if it isn't developed. They seek out responsive employees and seek out ways to develop them farther.

## Are Leaders Born or Made?

Almost every truly great leader will tell you that they developed over time and weren't born fully formed. Instead, the process of seeking challenges for self-transformation became critical for their development into the leaders that they eventually became.

Natural talent can only get you so far- it's the way you apply your talent that makes all the difference.

## *Key Takeaways*

• Companies that hire for talent alone create work cultures that value appearances over results, and often find themselves bankrupt.

• The mindset of a CEO is critical for setting the mindset of the entire organization they are running.

• Leaders are not born, they are developed through self-transformation and an ability to learn from challenges.

# CHAPTER 6
## *RELATIONSHIPS: MINDSETS IN LOVE (OR NOT)*

## Relationships Are Different

It's fairly easy to measure abilities like physical fitness and intelligence, but it's comparatively difficult to measure people's interpersonal skills. Some people even challenge whether or not this talent is an ability or just a way to be a good person. This makes it clear that as a society we don't fully understand relationship skills, and we have few tools in place for evaluating and improving these skills. This is one of the reasons why it can be so hard to maintain a growth mindset about the way we interact in our relationships. Without viewing them as a skill, it's hard to assume we can change them.

## Mindsets Falling in Love

Your mindset has a big impact on your romantic relationships. If you have a fixed mindset you will think that not only are you unable to change, your partner isn't able to either. Additionally, you will assume that the right relationship shouldn't be a lot of work, so the first hint of trouble might be enough for you to back out. A growth mindset would allow you to see both your partner and your relationship as a work in progress and something that can be continuously improved through effort and understanding.

## The Partner as Enemy

In the fixed mindset, your partner can quickly become your biggest enemy. Any failures on their part or in your relationship as a whole becomes a symbol of your innate flaws and becomes unbearable to live with. For every failure you need to attribute blame to either your permanent qualities or your partner's. It's little surprise your partner will get much of the blame.

Fixed mindsets put people on the defensive when a problem occurs, but a growth mindset lets you rise above the blame and try to fix the problem together.

## Competition: Who's The Greatest?

If you operate in a mindset where your abilities are measured once and become a defining characteristic of you, it makes sense you will constantly be in competition with others to try to be the best. This creates a toxic relationship dynamic when you feel like your partner has to constantly prove they are better than you.

## Developing Relationships

During the beginning of a relationship, you need to learn the skills necessary for coping with their differences, and to do this, the two of you need to feel that you are on the same side. A well-functioning relationship allows both partners to help each other develop, not change each other completely.

## Friendships

When it comes to the importance of mindset, friendships have a lot of similarities with partnerships. They create spaces for two people to validate each other and encourage their development, and we should seek out relationships that provide this in our lives. Don't spend your time investing in people who won't care about you or work to bring you down- rather find people who value what is good in you and work to bring it out more. Your failures and successes shouldn't threaten your friend's self-esteem. If they do, you need to evaluate those friendships.

## Shyness

Shyness brings out the opposite angle in relationships because shy people worry that others will judge or embarrasses them, and consequently bring them down. A fixed mindset prevents shy people from taking initiative and putting themselves out there because they see shyness as a fixed trait in themselves that can't be changed. Growth mindset shy people still get nervous during social interactions, but they have a resolve to push through their nerves because they know putting in the effort to meet new people is worth it. As an interaction goes on, growth minded people feel less shy and more comfortable, which causes them to make a better impression on the people they are talking to.

## Bullies and Victims: Revenge Revisited

Unfortunately, for many students getting bullied is a common occurrence in their daily lives, and schools are rarely able to do much to address it.

One thing that bullying victims can control is their mindset. The fixed mindset causes victims to feel deeply judged and as a flawed person ("they are picking on me because they know I'm worthless") while a growth minded victim looks at the bigger situation ("he's picking on me because his grades are bad and he feels insecure"). A growth mindset takes the power from the bully because it stops them from being able to define the worth of their victims.

### *Key Takeaways*

• For a happy relationship, keep a growth mindset about the kind of changes that your partner can make.

• The fixed mindset causes you to complete with your partner, not work with them.

• Children can handle bullying better when they try to understand their bully's situation.

# CHAPTER 7
# *PARENTS, TEACHERS AND COACHES: WHERE DO MINDSETS COME FROM?*

## Parents (and Teachers) Messages About Success and Failure

No loving parent or teacher ever intentionally tries to undermine the joy and discovery of learning in children, but unfortunately it still happens a lot. By focusing on results and success, parents and teachers can make it all about the results and stifle a desire for growth in children. For example, a mother who tells her daughter her painting shows how talented she is might be preventing her daughter from wanting to paint anything else, lest it not be as "talented" as her other work.

Focusing on results and not the journey to achieve them makes it difficult for students to value the work they put into it. If they are praised for being smart because they got their work in fast, what does it mean if they get their work in slow? Are they no longer smart?

## Teachers (and Parents): What Makes a Great Teacher? (Or Parent)

Lowering standards and giving unearned praise is a popular way of improving confidence in children, but it almost always backfires. How are over-coddled students supposed to handle criticism at their first job when they've been told their whole life how smart they are when they didn't have to try?

The best lesson that a parent or teacher can give students is to praise their efforts. Compliment how hard they worked and their ability to make improvements. Focus on traits that can be developed in them and not their natural abilities, and you will be encouraging to continue to achieve.

Don't let your praise become dependent on the results that they achieve. Rather, reassure them that their effort is the most valuable thing they can contribute and will pay off in the long run.

## Coaches: Winning Through Mindset

The effectiveness of a coach can vary, depending on what mindset they choose to operate under. A fixed mind-set coach values winning over everything else and equates the entire success or failure of the team on whether or not they are winning. Mistakes can be unbearable, so they strive to play games that are technically perfect even if that reduces the opportunity to take big risks that might pay off.

In contrast, a growth mindset coach values the contributions that each player can bring to the team. They are concerned with the ways their players can develop and strive to figure out what motivates each one to be their best. Less concerned with perfection, a growth mindset coach values progress that leads towards overall goals. By working their players harder than other coaches, they can ensure that their players approach each game well-prepared and ready to push themselves to the limit. Because growth minded coaches don't put limits on what their players can achieve, the results are often shockingly successful.

## Our Legacy

Parents, teachers and coaches have a big job to do. They are preparing the next generation to be confident in their abilities and not put limits on what they can achieve.

### *Key Takeaways*

• The language that parents, teachers and coaches use can have a big impact on the achievements of children.

• Focus on celebrating improvements, not successes.

# CHAPTER 8
## *CHANGING MINDSETS*

## The Nature of Change

So many of us have huge potential for accomplishing our dreams but become paralyzed by the effort of overcoming setbacks. In many cases, the simplest action or mindset change can make a huge difference in results, but without a growth mindset these changes can make us feel powerless and incapable.

But change is possible. By becoming aware of your mindset you can make the changes necessary to start living to your full potential.

## The Mindset Lectures

Dr. Dweck has seen firsthand through her college lectures what difference simply learning about the growth mindset can make in the lives of her students. The positive feedback that her students give her every year shows how much of an impact her teaching makes.

## A Mindset Workshop

Dr. Dweck's team has put together workshops for primary schools to study the impacts of teaching the growth mindset to students. Their work has shown that the students who learn to develop their growth mindset get better grades, show more enthusiasm for school and are more likely to attempt to tackle challenging math problems.

## Brainology

"Brainology" is a computer program created by Dr. Dweck's team to teach students how their brain takes in and retains information. After completing the game, students showed that they had learned more about how their brains took in information and were eager to put the study tips they learned into practice for their school work.

## More About Change

Addressing situations to create change can be difficult. Not only does change take a lot of effort, it can be emotionally taxing by making you vulnerable to failure. People tend to hold onto a fixed mindset because it's easier. They have an excuse every time they mess up to not learn from their mistakes and try again. But, making changes can be very rewarding. A growth minded student can learn more than they ever dreamed, and a growth minded athlete may find themselves playing for the pros someday.

Removing the limitations from your mind will help you to move forward and achieve everything you are capable of.

## Taking the First Step
Dr. Dweck provides a series of mental exercises that you can use to help you work through your fixed mindset reactions in order to come to a growth-mindset solution.

## People Who Don't Want to Change
Some people with a fixed mindset don't think the problem lies with them. They don't want to change and think that the problem is with the rest of the world's inability to change. It's easier to run away from their problems than to face their own weaknesses and work towards personal betterment.

## Changing Your Child's Mindset
It's very common for children to get trapped in a fixed mindset. You can help them by encouraging their efforts more than their results and getting them to see the connection between their efforts and the rewards of achievement.

## Mindset and Willpower
Making long term change can be so difficult that some people change their thinking to say that there is just a small problem they need to change that can be accomplished through willpower, not a total mindset change. They think they can make progress through sheer willpower and don't want to try anything else.

This is like students saying that if they are smart they will do well, regardless of the material or how much they study. It doesn't make sense! Without putting in concentrated effort, you can never expect to get better at what you don't already know.

## Maintaining Change
When people change their mindset, it can be difficult to maintain this progress because once the problem improves they stop doing what caused it to improve (having a growth mindset). Not only is this silly, it undermines the progress that they make. It's better to make a long term commitment to changing your mindset in order that the changes you make will last for the long term.

## The Road Ahead
Change is hard, there's no denying that. However, change is completely within your grasp if you decide to take the root of your problems seriously. By changing your mindset from a fixed thought pattern to a growth one, you will be working to solve many of your problems and pushing yourself to be your very best.

## ***END***

*If you enjoyed this summary, please leave an honest review on Amazon.com…it'd mean a lot to us!*

*Here are some other available titles from FastReads we think you'll enjoy:*

***Summary of Eat That Frog!*** 
**by Brian Tracy**

***Summary of How to Fail at Almost Everything and Still Win Big*** 
**by Scott Adams**

***Summary of Grit*** 
**by Angela Duckworth**

Made in the USA
Middletown, DE
27 June 2017